THE PAPER TREE

THE PAPER TREE

Caroline Goodwin

Caroline Goodwin

For Shina

Thank you so much
for reading!

Lyrics + Dirges
18 Sept 2019
Berkeley

BIG YES PRESS
San Luis Obispo, California

THE PAPER TREE

Cover art: pashabo/shutterstock.com

Library of Congress Cataloging-in-Publication Data
Goodwin, Caroline
The Paper Tree: poems / by Caroline Goodwin

ISBN 978-0-9896366-6-7

Book Design by Sylvia Aranda
Printing by KC Book Manufacturing
Poet Portrait by Darin Boville

BIG YES PRESS
PO Box 4344 San Luis Obispo, California 93403 USA
www.bigyespress.com

ACKNOWLEDGEMENTS

These poems appeared or were publicly presented at the following:

"At Mavericks," *Aperçus Quarterly*, January 2017.

"The River Eyot" "Aurora" and "When the Rain" *Canary*, Winter 2017.

"Fireweed" "Back Street" "Hinge" "Text Me, Ishmael" and an
early version of "Goat Women" can be found in an online poetry
chapbook exchange in the manuscript, *Grasslands*, San Francisco
State University Poetry Center.

"Rana Draytonii" "Mission Blue" and "When the Rain" were presented at
Redwood City, San Mateo County Board of Supervisors meetings, 2016.

"Underfoot" *Brain Mill Press Voices Blog*, April, 2016.

"Mission Blue" *Canary*, Spring, 2016.

"Back Street" *Samizdat Literary Journal*, 10/2013.

"Fireweed" and "Text Me, Ishmael" *sparkle + blink*, November, 2013.

"Fireweed" *The Witness Anthology*, JackLeg Press, 2012.

"Text Me, Ishmael" Literary Pocket Book Series #2,
Pontypridd, Wales, UK, 2012.

NOTES TO MY READERS

My maternal grandparents were Presbyterian educators who moved from Iowa to the small island town of Sitka, Alaska in 1923. There, they worked at Sheldon Jackson School, raised five children and spent sixty years of married life until my grandmother's death in 1983. While I was born and raised in Anchorage, my childhood visits to Sitka remain clear and powerful in my memory.

According to the essay "On Migrations" by Andrew Hope III, published in 2000 in *Will the Time Ever Come? A Tlingit Sourcebook*, "the name Sitka is derived from the Tlingit Sheey.at'iká, 'the outer edge of a branch pointing downward, with knotholes running through,' a poetic description of the area's topography."

Throughout my life, I have had the privilege of learning from people whose ancestors have lived in Sitka for thousands of years and who have devoted their lives to preserving their culture. Many of the poems in *The Paper Tree* are firmly rooted in Sitka, where I aim to investigate both personal and historical trauma, and the connections between the two. Through imagery and sound, I hope to play a small part in mourning several members of the community and to celebrate the important cultural work that is done behind the scenes and outside of the spotlight.

I give a heartfelt THANK YOU to Big Yes Press, for their faith in my work, their time and their dedication to poetry.

Caroline Goodwin
January, 2017

for Nick Goodwin

my rock and my star

rest in peace

I love you

and for the Sitka Brady Bunch

with gratitude

The carver leans toward me,
"Does wind around Raven sculpt Raven,
or does Raven sculpt the wind around himself?
Do the tide flats emerge,
or is that Tide Woman pulling back her blanket?
What matters is not what's left to the eye,
but what's taken away."

Robert Davis Hoffman, "Carving"
Village Boy: Poems of Cultural Identity

Table of Contents

FIREWEED

Shellmound   17
Back Street   18
Little Creek   20
Fireweed   21

BLACK OAK

Letting   30
Mission Blue   32
At Mavericks   34
Goat Women   35
Aurora   36
Creekside   37
Glass Dove   40
Hinge   43
For Rebekah   44
Rana Draytonii   47
When the Rain   48

MARIGOLD

Text Me, Ishmael   50

BIRCH

Horseback   56
Underfoot   57
The Paper Tree   63
The Mrytle Tree   66
The River Eyot   68
At Starrigavin   69

FIREWEED

SHELLMOUND

Down the rivers. Down the long
afternoon where she lay in the dead
leaves downwind, around town. Bough
bearing petals, bearing the ghost
girl in black leather, pickup truck.
Just under the surface, a sprinkling
of shells and of dust. Hush, the wind,
the falling light. Her hands in soil,
wet bank, gold reeds where
shining seeds and arrowheads
reside. Where the roots take hold.
Where a screech owl stands
guard over the clearing through the night.
Downwind from King Mountain,
a storm coming up off the Gulf,
Fourth Avenue, Covenant House.
An eighteen-wheeler grinds uphill, piled
high with old growth. And the silt
beds, the cottonwoods, the riverbank.
Her tongue is a down feather caught
in one branch. Then the old moon,
the moon that is always rising, always
placing one cold finger in that landscape,
finding the dust and the girl, ghost
girl in the hollow, her hands
opening, fan-shaped, the clear bones,
the grass pressed flat, the whole
place held forever just like that.

BACK STREET

for Isabella Grace (Sing) Brady
February 18, 1924 - April 23, 2012

bush poppy   tower of jewels
        hatchling in the leaves   in
the old shed   my shears and blades
        your cedar canoe   how quickly

you walked up the hill   the old
        stovetop and sourdough   beads
in hanks   the greenish glass   your daughter
        at the tideline building castles

for the crabs   purple shore   afterlight
        dogrose blinking pink along the river
the fish skin   hook song   halibut eye   silver
        scales coating our arms

silver sky drawn tight over the village
        man with dog   man with hair to his waist
and the ocean hunched along the street
        tipping and spilling   my cedar root

basket   painted house and the air filled with salt
          crab pots and rope   the sidewalk moss
and the new cedar handmade casket   plastic
          rose   goat hair and leather

I miss you   I have seen your face amongst the
          grasses at the back of the house   thimble-
berry and wild carrot   blue painted pottery
          shard I glue to a metal pin and wear
                    against my heart

LITTLE CREEK

sparkling and willow
and rock face gray gravel

crouching

under my boot
the dried green

early light breaking
stitching itself
into the nest
into the falcon
gripping fur

my footprint and shapes
the water takes

how long will I stand here
watching

the room of light
the hopsice bed
the green glass float
the breath

a little scissors
held loosely
and close

FIREWEED

for Jennifer Brady-Morales
August 21, 1952 - July 20, 2012

i.

it was dawn   there were thrushes
up and down the path   moss
gathering the light   gathering
the rain and the men hauling in
the nets   the nets filled with silver
coins   jewels   oil   an abundance

there was the frost waiting in the mountaintops
and we wanted to show you
all the crystals that stood underneath the needles
waiting   they were waiting for you
to notice them and take them in hand

ii.

how long had you been gazing
west   how many afternoons

did you see his face   did you want to touch
his face   was he waiting   did you ask

him to bring you   did you request
your own canoe   (how neatly it cuts

through the channel)   were you hopeful
did you ask   were we wrong about everything
were we

iii.

everything waking up now as it always
does   fern   hillock   hummock
root wad   tide pool   and a hairline fracture
where the light crawls along

and the spines and the moss after nightfall
and the faces of the women
lining the riverbed   holding out their baskets
one by one by one by one

they step up to the trunk
where the water shines and the tiny
root hairs reach into the cold
invisible   like nerves

iv.

nothing could hold the salt nothing could capture the paint
nothing could hold the wind nothing could cover the stones

v.

did he say it did he touch you did he call
was he there did you believe him was there
smoke were there rattles were there teeth
did you ask did the blanket hide you
did the wind spill through the channel
did the ice feel right were there matches
were there needles could we have spoken
better could we have held you tighter
could the light have traveled any more
quickly into your heart

vi.

afterwards   we could see him traveling
through the village   we didn't want
to see him   we didn't want to see

but he just kept limping along there
and sometimes he stopped at the window
and we closed the blinds

and he tapped and he tapped with a fingernail
a mussel shell
a piece of fish
a cup of oil
a twisted bone
a hunk of wood
an ivory goose
a thorny grin
and we opened the window after all

vii.

there were the baskets and bowls
and blankets and your daughter carried the nets
and the nets kept filling up   we couldn't stop them
(her wrists adorned with silver and garnet)
and when we gathered at the roadside

there was light
there was ice and rain
there was the sound of the ice
touching down onto the earth

and there were the thrushes
there were the songs
all along the path
and there was your voice

twisted into the woven leaves
we were sure of it

BLACK OAK

LETTING

and evening arrived completely
      unlovely with its white leaves
and a joyful noise and you   mother
      bending over the raised bed   salmonberry

thorns at the edge   at your small knees
      a basket for gathering   a row
of branches blowing away
      behind you   all the petals moving

they are the darkest pink   filled
      with vessels and a spiral center
gold eye   shaped like the old spirals
      carved in the rock face in the door

of the herring house   frozen throat
      pink black   stuck on the high point
of the red alder   stuck in my heart
      and my fingers   my own sister

her hair cropped short and shiny
      leaving us and offering every cell
to the mud   every bead of spit   dry shell
      and solstice and the corner house

draped in red lights   the sound
          of the berries of the dogwood
and hemlock and cedar and birch
          the twig nest   blue-black jelly

and wine saying *hush* saying
          hush now   bright end of the yard
pale fiddlehead and a needle of sunset
          a green leaf   it is almost June

it is almost time   rain on the seedlings
          on the trowel and switch
alongside the house   the ripening jar
          of fish eggs and potato

and the red bark   yellow bark
          white bark in the sun and
the old Russian cross and spring and
          my mother's small song

MISSION BLUE

for San Bruno Mountain

I go up before sunrise   before the light
        finds the promenade and salt flats
and marina   the baylands and lagoon
        alive with willows and goldeneye

before the door opens in the east
        and the night shift clocks out
and the parents and older brothers and sisters
        come home to the younger ones

to wake them and prepare the first
        meal of the day   my own mind
opening into the familiar   into the old
        grief blue as a glacier

I go up   and when light reaches
        clear water at the center
of every lupine   when blue wings come
        like a blessing to cover my eyes

there is my grandfather
       leaving the garden   offering
bright lettuce and the formula
       for a good crop—one starfish under every

potato and a layer of herring eggs in March —
       hand over his heart   hand
placing the last rose   the sun opening
       over the bay   into the stonecrop

into the blue wings we all hold onto there

AT MAVERICKS

we stride along the harbor   baby
        in the frontpack   sea lions

lolling about on sailboat decks and you
        husband   wading into the green

lines in the sky   these gulls and kites
        and the old *scree scree*

and the baby   blue night   a few
        days tossed into the mix

into the distance   redwoods
        blurring   a carpet of roots

high nest of the murrelet
        wingbeat   back and forth

a white smear a high note
        a rusty hinge   a cradle

me there   bowl of my ribs
        of my mouth   my breath

counted out—all day it blooms
        between my teeth

GOAT WOMEN

Long hairs on the legs give the animal
the appearance of wearing pantaloons.

They called us names. They said sensitive
they said weak and yanked on our hair and
walked into the house and glanced
into the pot on the stove and said
what the hell is that shit on a shingle?

They thought we were simply the tufts of snow
on Arrowhead Peak, so we shifted
a little every now and again to prove
we were alive. Then we gathered
ourselves and came down.
In June we grew horns.

In October we strung our own hairs together
to make the longest threads and we took the old loom
down from the attic and breathed into the sheets
of metal to make a million plates
and when we dedicated every winter night to sewing
new coats of mail they said nice work.

They strode in their boots to the end of the pier.
We watched from dry land, licking our hooves and laughing
when boats took shape on the horizon. We knew
how fine life was up on the peak, that we were always
warm and strong together holding up the world.

AURORA

Pinpoints and dust motes.
        Emerald pincushion
on the windowsill. Fabric
        over the sky-light.
Moss blowing in a high tree.
        In a shadow in a hand.
A child lifting a stone.
        Tide pool and hermit crab.
Giant green anemone. Shore light
        and mantlepiece. Photo
box made of birch-bark. Photo
        of garment and seam.
Of the fireside and
        frenzied moth. Silver
wing. Silver needle through a blue
        bead after the last fish is cleaned.

CREEKSIDE

In September the tiny gold frogs
chirped in the meadow, hopped
onto my arms and left a sheen.

And when I walked out the door
at last, they remained. Invisible,
so cool, a kind of sleeve
a kind of scent or open

space where even the skinny
purplish willows shine.
Where the light tips
aside, takes on new shapes

and a grey cloud descends
in the wee hours
to whisper into the chest.

How many times have I felt
it now, and turned away?

And yet it persists, in the small pieces, in the gold wool the blue wool
the tatters, the garden flags where I can feel it waking, waking early,
rosemary buckling down in raised beds, the neighbor cats leaving small
tufts of tail fur along the gutters, pricklebush and corner store and sky,
pearl gray, abalone—what vision what memory poking hard : sternum,
fever, blue vein, strong tongue, strong verb, bitter root, screw.

GLASS DOVE

calling out
    brown thrasher
        jackhammer
bramble black
    cobweb
        over my window
this pulsing
    in a lamb's ear
        in my cheek
pale pink
    morning clouds
        lithe and light
glacier blue
    a torn hole
        a girl's voice
into the heavens
    into the choir
        her hands at
her hands at
    her warbling
        skyward
skylark and phoebe
    white weasel
        hoary marmot
hunched in the woodpile
    spider leg and moth wing
        and the shapes

of the succulents
> the slick pearls
>> beetle rock

and a light crack
> dawn crack antenna
>> in the reeds

and the rushes
> and the grasses
>> the cattails

where the green
> sharpens its blades
>> where the bottleneck

jagged edge
> water skin
>> heals over

surface tension
> membrane
>> hostess of silver

light finding the blood
> edge and thorn
>> and infinite

splitting   rust-red
> holding
>> an ivory button

and all the orange poppies
> on my shelf
>> are believing

now the spikes
       the shapely
              glass
fractured
       the segmented
              tailfeather and beak
the follicle and palm
            I hold it out
I hold it up
       my pocketful
            my pocketful
my pocketful of ice

HINGE

the moon is no gate   but a silver
       charm   fastened tight
and swiveling on its hinge
       at the mountain shoulder
down which it tumbles
       into my lap   where it sparks
and flickers

where it ignites the old
       lantern I set at the end
of the lane   a face in every
       window   white
diamond   blue knot   little
       piles of silver shavings

in the ditch   and my longing
       suspended in glass
in the hole through which
       the needle passes
and passes again   *come here*
       come here   I am
calling   singing   sweeping
       soot into the pan
come you indoors   come back

FOR REBEKAH

friend
there is
nothing like this bay
     quiet fern
cool spot on the back
     of the hand

tonight the water's surface
     reflects the smokey-rose
and the day passes and what
     can i show for it?

oh cone-bearing
     incense cedar
western yew and birch
     and a bright gold band

on clamshell and thistle
     this flycatcher
that turkey vulture circling the valley

where we ascend the old
stairs   the lichen at work
     at its trumpets and cups
and lobes

and we set out to explore
　　　　　our own thoughts　two
friends at their desks

two juncos in the alders
　　　　　a few lines of a poem
and what reveals itself

rose-shaped　so slowly　in the mind　in
　　　　　the daylight bending away

RANA DRAYTONII (California Red-Legged Frog)

for my hands also held him
for he was dry and tiny at the edge of the pond
      where the mud shone
for the rain arrived with the tides and it filled my dreams
      and in my dreams we gazed into our own skulls
for the poem rose up the tree trunk
for paint held the dust motes and pigment
      and the young man painted an owl on the bricks
      and it was good
for there were the torn clouds
      and sea lavender   the purple stems
for behind the white latticework the weeds glowed
      and a light arrived from the coast
      and the hissing was high in the cypress
for he also held me in his hands
for the end of life is nothing
for a fragrant sage blew in from the desert
      and the hummingbird and woodpecker made
         their sounds in the lane
for the man on the corner in the twilight
for the bluish smoke
for he called to my beloved on the other side
      and i nearly sensed her

for the turtle in the ocean filled with eggs
for the burrs and the weeds
for the shape of feathers
       and the ways in which they feel
              against the skin
for their fine hooks and barbs
for he dies every day of starvation
       and of thirst and of abandonment
for the ways in which we take our leave are manifold and
       growing
for the sound of his voice was like nothing
       and was like everything
for the soil held it all rotting
for the flame and the bowl of fresh water
for the music of the pearly throat
       and the pond that finally
              called us all by name

WHEN THE RAIN

when we watch over the beach
        over the snowy plover
seeking shelter in the couch grass
        with our hands opening
to the west and forget ourselves
        in the narrow corridor in
filaments of sunlight that remain

when we detect the first
        dry leaves
along the pavement
scratching at our arms
        and remember the blood
in ferguson   in jasper   in iguala
        in our streets   the trees
lighting up our living rooms with silver

tinsel and ornaments   when we drink
        the clear water   clean water
the sky returning to its feathered
        clouds and stillness and we come out
let us come out with our eyes open
        and with our hearts prepared for both
the battle and the feast

MARIGOLD

TEXT ME, ISHMAEL

i.

Ability to evaluate different genres of creative writing.
Linked-In, Jim has switched from the Higher
Education Industry to the Insurance Industry.
Transferable skills. Your inner child galloping
along the rocky ridge. Did you happen
to catch the YouTube of the man trying
to cross Halibut Point Road? So intoxicated
he finally lies down and rolls. Himalayan poppies
lining the wall, and huge marigolds under the window-
sill. Breaking dawn, after another night,
the husband trudges out into the morning's
mouth. He's bending at the stern of the vessel,
he's hauling in the nets. What does he bring
home through the door in the evening? What skill set?

ii.

The hill is made of Old Red Sandstone
from the Devonian Period. Out of the fort
at Crug Hywel, the tiny iron figures marched
onto your windowsill, bearing knives and bayonets.
In the mean time, we brewed some strong tea.
And inside the chambers of our hearts, matchsticks
formed the figures of men. Our sister
crumpled in the ditch. Old friend, they lay you flat
upon the table and lifted out the sour parts. And your new
life began. Your children still clung to your hips;
they did not know the difference. And I lit the lantern
in the evening and I set out the bowls of seeds.
Inside the greenhouse, under the wrinkled glass,
our sister is standing up and dressing herself.

iii.

Always trudging out into the morning's
mouth. Out through the front door and up
the coast, across the seedlings, the artichokes.
Goldfinches nesting in the hedge. Galloping
child, hopeful daughter, friend request. There,
the fringe is eaten away by moths. And there,
bright snowberries decorate the creek. What
smooth beast? Asters and geranium, a horse
struggling in a ditch. Imagine that we had a long
enough rope and the strength. That the carousel
never stopped turning, the bright eyes and manes. How
different each morning, and how long would you keep
hauling it in, planting the pumpkins, gathering the fleece?
Listen. The looms are clicking and thumping, wool
pulled thin and looking for a place.

iv.

Our sister, crumpled in the ditch. Months
for the bruise to disappear, green lake
filling up under a long flat sky.
The surface looked as though it would spill
right over... and we stared and stared but
did not know any strategy with which
to contain it. Lots of times they do remain
behind bars. We thought about the shadows
marching across the men's faces. Not how
to manage the fear or the tendency to return.
Far away, several bottlenose dolphins headed
for the West Coast at breakneck speed, carrying
radiation from the spill. And somewhere else a hand
stroked a harp. And our sister chewed the little pill.

v.

Linked-In, over the shining trees. A flock
of sandpipers breaks apart, reunites, breaks
apart again. In Fort Collins, the fire took
more than 82,000 acres, 191 homes, 1 human
life. Still, the tide rose and fell. I wanted
to hold you, to reinvent the old rooms filled
with one scent. I spent a year walking
the shore. I lifted the stone, I stuck my head
deep into the pool, peeked around in there. Cool
water, still water. The giant green anemone
fastening itself to the driftwood, rough
as sandpaper, waving and reaching, every tentacle
filled with nerves. And the mouth. Big flower.
I wanted to bring it home but I left it there.

BIRCH

HORSEBACK

my daughter in the saddle   the hills
not rising behind her   not coming up   not
jutting into the sky but   rather
holding her like a couple
of large soft arms
as the animal turns
at the far end of the fence and heads
back toward me   I am standing at the gate now
and I can sense the valves of my heart opening
and thumping shut   steady as hooves   unbeautiful
as a thing you'd find beneath a stump
something mysterious and unidentifiable
with jagged edges   asymmetrical   black or perhaps a dark
purple   maybe the size of a fist   (like they say)
but so distinct from anything you've ever
seen before that you're moved to invent
a new kingdom   a realm untouched
by the physical world
where the need to name the shape
does not even exist
and nothing can be pinned
down or held as evidence and nobody
knows the code or holds the key

UNDERFOOT

all mist and movement

my daughter
is messing with her hair
with her new
body
at the mirror

old dog
warming my sleep

and a memory
held between
the fingertips

your heart and lungs
the shining reeds

fill with grey sun
with lichen stone

if I scrub the linens
if I apply the mask
brush out the knots
            —oh
dusty banjo
your voice
a spider leg a
hummingbird wing

at the edge of the playground the ice was forming its beautiful shapes and crackling up under a black spruce where I could tell that it wanted to love me that it could not did not love me but there were all sorts of voices roaming around in the sunlight in the crystals and I caught one and dropped it into my pocket I can still hear it burning there

envy
the garden
a white rose
browning

photograph
serrated leaf

and it was early
when I followed him
into the language
into the circle of men

river walk and thin leaf my alder my rhododendron fungus and canker
and salmonberry ghost in and out of the gold leaves with my button
jar with my jam jar jelly jar pie tin the ground is the same ground
moving and loving and the faraway roar of the river I walk in the
dieback root rot duff and sweet humus in my skin in my palms my spine
my heart alone afraid I am just a kid myself in the autumn in the
leafmold the shame the detritus

with my thick hide

and smoke
the censer
huffing
beardtongue
a certain
violet

chanting

daughter
your slim waist

is the garden
arriving

THE PAPER TREE

daughter, in
      the morning
            i sweep
the front porch
      for your feet, soft
and dry

and i slip the lavender
      into a green
vase, tie a ribbon
      of your hair and
one bead

one blue bead
      the shape
of your first
      tooth lost

were you to join your sisters
were you to lie down under the wheels

the old plate lifted
        out of the cupboard
scrapes the wood
        scrapes my wrist
repeating the sky
        and the meadows
and the story
filling
        with wild rose
with the fragrant gold
        bread
        under my hands
and the angels

in the evening
        when the back
                porch hosts
these enormous brambles
        when i try but
                they are very
strong
        their shining stems
the color of blood
        their thorns metallic

their leaves filled
        with the toughest
thing -- a chain or a system
        of stitches

        were you to wake in time to see them
        were you to actually wake

to the bluebirds
        at the fence
        to the one bruised
larkspur
        against the window

against the wind
        a single drop of
nectar in the pistil
        in the receptacle

to the truth and the chisel

i would contain you
deep in the peach-white bark

THE MYRTLE TREE

i hear the buzz   the highway
  breathing   trains
  and a joyful noise and you   father
standing alongside the rails
  the row of pencils in your pocket
your large brown shoes   a crate of oranges
  and a host of shadows falling away
behind you all the boxcars moving they
  are filled with faces   filled with singing

and the song is an old one
  like the song of wind in the myrtle
or the song of the waiting insects
  the articulated thorax   blue black
moving through the city on rails
  moving through my heart and lungs
my church on the hill in winter
stained glass and incense   shining regalia

every crystal in the snowbank
  every flake of ice   freezing wind
tinsel and the solstice and the corner
house draped in blue lights   song
  of the bee wings and hornet
  and wasp and yellow jacket
paper nest and horsetail

saying *hush* saying *hush now*
      at the shadow end of the barn
      tiny legs in a cobweb
and a little sunlight   the bluing wood   it is almost
      december   it is almost time   frost
on the ties   on the rails and the freight   alongside
      my house the sleeping
      currant and raspberry cane and wolf willow

the red bark   yellow bark white bark
      in the sun and
my grandfather with his song
      and my father whose arms
came out of the myrtle tree
      and held me through that night

THE RIVER EYOT

child at the circle
drawn in mud   willow
branch and shining fur—

humming under the surface
earwig and pillbug
cranefly and pearl—

heron at the tideline
stock-still, clam shell, thin
white lines, milk-thistle, quill—

hold out your hands
open your heart
here's where the world slides in

AT STARRIGAVIN

for Arlene Gamble (May 27, 1961 - March 14, 2012)
for Lael Grant (April 2, 1979 - October, 2012)

I will sing you
on the outside
edge of a branch
pointing south
burning mouth
burning gray
concentric
lichen

spirals
and undertow
and image of gills
of red-black
silk, torn
silk, ruby-
red patches
of silk afloat
in the river
in the silver

vessels
turning back
with their catch
with their kings
their lines

rolled up in metal
spools
and hitches
the men wiping
their hands
their lips
and pulling on
their cotton gloves
and rowing

So I wake up to clear this light snow from the front steps. Thin clouds down over the mountains will receive it. There is a variety of ways in which the surface of the skin reflects the sky. In my garden a little bit of you. *Three years after the disappearance her family has asked the state to issue a death certificate.* A knuckle of driftwood.

I will hold you
blonde light
        cupped
in the palm

belonging
        to god

to the cut
        crystal

when you sit
across the table
let me reach

oh crooked
river

So the song loops through the skies. The slivers of weathered wood Old man at a goathide, a grizzly sow and two cubs at the river mouth. Pointed horn. Red moon rising. Over the reeds a layer of tiny gray feathers. A fur hat and a hump of kinnikinnik, brown petals. An abalone tray. I saw a tiny ball of wax stuck to the edge it was like a vortex or a new star it almost had a face and a voice. A miniscule spot on the lung. I tried to pinch it, I tried to hide it in my pocket with the blue dust.

I will sing you
I will warble
my old lady
pledge
at the smokehouse
door:

answer only
to the salmonberry
dye and sparkling
thorn
the dried fish
ivory needle
and a drop
of light--

where you are lifting
you are shaking
the entire
black
channel
around your
shoulders
like a cloak

In a button in a locket, a minus tide, a jingle shell, the old brown
bottles and riprap and courthouse, dryrot and a film of rain on my
cheeks, lean-to, folded paper box, burn marks on the wrist, on copper
on steeple on wild celery on goosetongue on crab pot on rope
on seaweed on brush, on the seastar on the sunstar, on that tremendous
heaped-up peach-colored sunset cloud between us (to the west) through
the silver space, alongside the vessels, sailing back.

I will sing you I
will hold up your
turquoise bead
and found red hat
some winter light
in my gauzy
              curtains
when december
is the water sheet
closing over
eye and cheek
is a knife
sharpening itself
is the arc
the skiff took
back at the land

the starfish
the lanternfish
the swim bladder
and shell
and shining kelp
so cold (dark)
so quick
and peaceful
land rolling
green rolling out
under my feet

FURTHER NOTES

"Back Street" is dedicated to Tlingit Culture-Bearer Isabella Brady (Yeidikook'aa, Kiks.adi of the Point House). Isabella was born in Sitka, Alaska in 1924 and raised by her grandfather, Peter Simpson, who was known as the Father of Alaska Native Land Claims and of the civil rights organization, the Alaska Native Brotherhood. A woman of deep Christian faith, Isabella was one of the first Alaska Native women to earn a college degree. She founded the Sitka Native Education Program in 1974 so that Native youth could learn about their culture and gain a positive self-image. It was her vision to preserve Tlingit songs, dances, stories, language and traditions. During her lifetime, Isabella received many awards, including the Tlingit and Haida Living Cultural Treasure Award and the Jamestown College Hall of Fame. She served countless terms as President and Chaplain of the Alaska Native Sisterhood Camp #4 and began the Sitka Community Dinners for Thanksgiving and Christmas so that "people who didn't have anywhere else to go would have somewhere to enjoy a meal." Her family meant the world to her; she is survived by her children Barbara, Ralph, Louise and Judy Brady and adopted children James Swift, Eileen Gallagher and Vicki D'Amico, eighteen grandchildren and twenty-two great-grandchildren.

"Fireweed" is dedicated to Isabella's daughter Jennifer Brady (Ts'enak, Kiks'adi of the Point House). Jennifer, born in 1952, was the second eldest of Bill and Isabella Brady's five children, and the mother of Steven and Vanessa Brady-Morales. She received her associate of arts degree from Sheldon Jackson Junior College and went on to study under various renowned Northwest Coast artists in Alaska and Canada. She was known for her extraordinary carvings and design work in wood, gold and silver, drum-making and other media. She worked in a variety of settings, with patience and encouragement, and was well-respected by her peers. To quote a co-worker in human services, "The clients had a distinct respect for Jennifer as a Native counselor and her ability to actively listen, providing them a safe environment that was conducive to healing and recovery. Those of us that got to work with her were touched by her gentle spirit, her eagerness to learn and her dedication and commitment to providing the best services to the clients." The poem takes its title from a wild plant in the evening primrose family that grows extensively in the temperate Northern Hemisphere. It is known as a "pioneer species"—one that returns quickly after a disturbance to the land such as a fire.

Caroline Goodwin moved from Alaska to the San Francisco Bay Area in 1999 to attend Stanford as a Wallace Stegner Fellow in poetry. Her books are *Kodiak Herbal* (2008), *Gora Verstovia* (2010), *Text Me, Ishmael* (2012), *Trapline* (2013) and *Peregrine* (2015). She lives on the San Mateo coast with her two daughters and teaches at the Stanford Writer's Studio and California College of the Arts. From 2014 - 2016 she served as the first Poet Laureate of San Mateo County.

www.carolinegoodw.com